Loch Lomond, Stirling & Trossachs

and the Forth Valley

Photography by Colin Baxter

Text by Gilbert Summers

LOMOND BOOKS

EDINBURGH · SCOTLAND

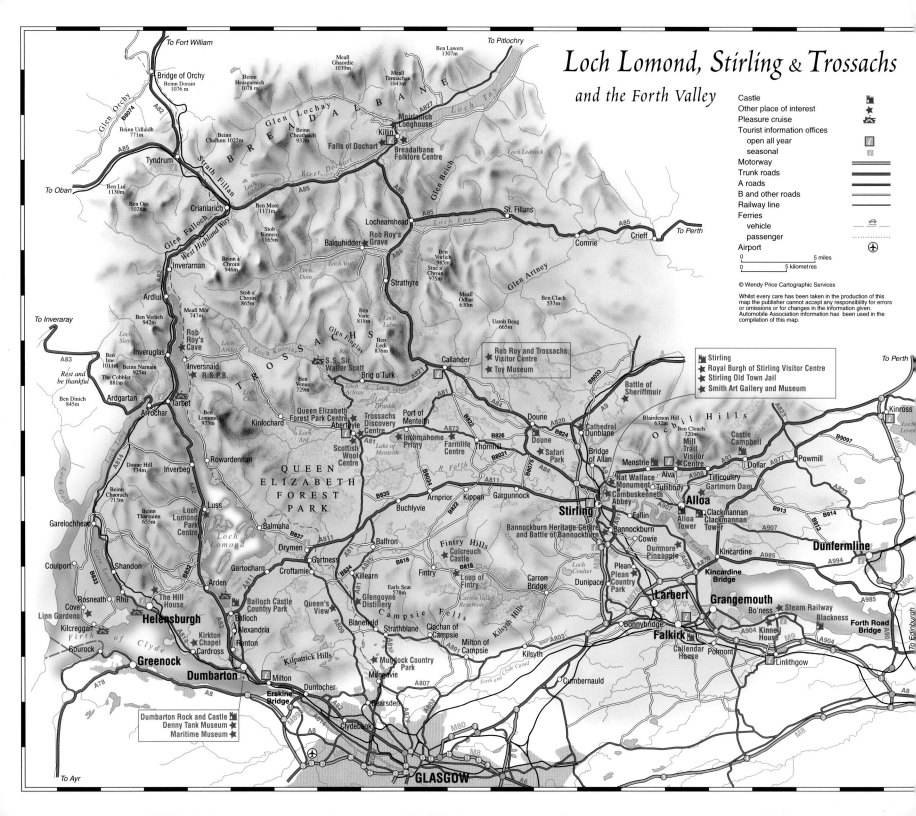

Loch Lomond, Stirling & Trossachs
and the Forth Valley

Castle
Other place of interest
Pleasure cruise
Tourist information offices
   open all year
   seasonal
Motorway
Trunk roads
A roads
B and other roads
Railway line
Ferries
   vehicle
   passenger
Airport

0   5 miles
0   5 kilometres

© Wendy Price Cartographic Services

Whilst every care has been taken in the production of this map the publisher cannot accept any responsibility for errors or omissions or for changes in the information given. Automobile Association information has been used in the compilation of this map.

Rob Roy and Trossachs Visitor Centre
Toy Museum

Stirling
Royal Burgh of Stirling Visitor Centre
Stirling Old Town Jail
Smith Art Gallery and Museum

Dumbarton Rock and Castle
Denny Tank Museum
Maritime Museum

Loch Lomond, Stirling & Trossachs
and the Forth Valley

CONTENTS

Loch Lomond, Stirling & Trossachs

Introduction

Touching the shores of the Forth in the east and the Clyde in the west, this area straddles Scotland and lies both above and below the line where Highland and Lowland meet. It also takes in two locations more strongly associated with tourism than just about anywhere else in Scotland. Firstly, the famed beauties of Loch Lomond have gone around the world in song. Scotland's largest loch (in terms of its surface area), along with its bonnie banks, has become a kind of byword for Scottish scenery. Though some might argue there are other lochs that are bonnier, Loch Lomond had a head start in the popularity stakes: it lies close to main population centres and is comparatively easy to reach.

Much the same could be said for that other famous name, the Trossachs. Though no two guidebooks will ever quite agree on the definition of the area, this particular craggy swathe of forest and loch, centred on the narrow pass leading down to Loch Katrine, has attracted visitors seeking the picturesque since at least the end of the eighteenth century.

Stirling, the area's main town, also has a claim to fame. In the days long before huge estuary-spanning bridges, or the technology to drain marshlands, this town with its castle on a high rock controlled the roads between Lowland and Highland. Its vital strategic position earned it the title 'the key to Scotland', a reference to former more war-like times. It is no coincidence that the Battle of Bannockburn, which secured Scotland's independence from England for almost four centuries, was fought within sight of the walls of the fortress at Stirling.

At places like Stirling, Gaelic-speaking Highlander met Lowland-dwelling Sassenach (Gaelic: southerner). Two cultures came into contact – and not always amicably, as tales of cattle-stealing and skirmishes in the villages nearby reveal. For example, no traveller in the Stirling and Trossachs area can avoid meeting up with Rob Roy MacGregor. This tartan Robin Hood figure not only boosted the area's tourism figures in the 1990s thanks to his Hollywood portrayal, but has also become a kind of symbol for the clash of cultures which really did take place right up to the time the clan system of the Highlands broke down. Hereabouts, Highland tribe met Lowland commerce and industry. This theme was taken up by Sir Walter Scott in his novel *Rob Roy*, mostly set in the Aberfoyle area on the very edge of the Highlands.

This Highland-Lowland contrast is the key to the whole area. By the late eighteenth century and the beginnings of the Romantic age, attitudes changed to the wild and 'uncivilised', Highlands. A kind of cult of the picturesque developed, which is

BEN LOMOND (opposite), in the distance, translates as the beacon hill.

ROB ROY MACGREGOR (below), the notorious cattle trader, cattle thief and blackmailer, roamed the Trossachs some 300 years ago.

HIGHLAND
MEETS
LOWLAND –
Loch Lomond's
islands and Conic
Hill looking east
along the fault line.

still with us today. The nearness to the relatively crowded central belt of Scotland meant that its beauties were soon opened up to tourists. Today, Callander and Aberfoyle, the Trossachs' two gateways, are busy right through the year, while the cruising grounds of the sea-lochs and the Clyde estuary west of Loch Lomond also play their part in an area where recreation has for long been important.

The main impression of the area, this Highland-Lowland split, is also very conspicuous in landscape terms. Geologists call it the Highland Boundary Fault. The line where the tough rocks of the Highlands meet the softer Lowlands runs down in a south-westerly direction from the edges of the Grampians far to the north-east. It passes close to Ben Ledi – the hill which seems to loom at the end of the main street of Callander – and goes on through the Trossachs by Aberfoyle. Then it goes through Conic Hill by Balmaha on the east bank of Loch Lomond. It also cuts over the hills to Helensburgh and through the Clyde to the island of Bute.

Time and time again, the visitor will have the sense of approaching a different country: for example, as road and river are squeezed together in close proximity at the Pass of Leny just above Callander; or as the main road towards Aberfoyle runs due north, then just beyond this gateway community, becomes the Duke's Road and zig-zags up the steep wall of the fault line into the heart of the Trossachs itself. Yet another notable moment in exploring this area is when the panorama opens out at the Queen's View on the A809 Drymen-Milngavie road to reveal the northward glitter of Loch Lomond and the long ramparts of endless mountains.

Below the fault line are plenty of essentially Lowland communities – places like Killearn and Balfron, tending to look towards Glasgow, just a few miles further to the south. However, such is the area's geological complication, that it would be misleading to suggest that the hills actually stop south of the Highlands. The Campsie Fells and Fintry Hills, also the Kilsyth Hills, and, most conspicuously, the Ochil Hills east of Stirling, are like dislocated chunks of the Highlands. They shelter their own little communities, or, in the case of the Ochil Hills, have provided both swift-flowing burns and upland pasture to support a textile industry which still functions today.

Falkirk is an historically important town in the Forth Valley. This is due to its location between the

Forth and the Clyde and its proximity to Edinburgh and Stirling. Some remains of the Roman Antonine Wall survive close to the town especially at the fort of Rough Castle. Falkirk was also the site of the largest livestock tryst (cattle market) in Scotland. In the mid-nineteenth century, 300,000 head of cattle and the same number of sheep were driven from the Highlands and sold here. At the same time, the giant Carron Company's iron foundries provided the chief industry.

To the north, where the mountains close in, the former strongholds of the Gael are still much to the scenic taste of today's visitor. The northernmost part of this area – from around Killin westwards to Tyndrum – is known as Breadalbane. A rock type fairly rich in minerals gives the Breadalbane mountains their characteristic grey and green look in spring and summer. Bright with upland grasses and alpine plants in high season (notably in the Ben Lawers area above Loch Tay), in autumn these hills take on a more russet tone and are less heathery in appearance than in many parts of the Highlands to the north.

From the modern-day visitor's point of view, it is inevitable that an area which has been involved with the tourism industry for two centuries has a well-developed infrastructure: in short, it looks after its tourists very well. Fortunately, it is also large and grand enough not to appear over-run in high season. For all its popularity, there are still wild and lonely places to discover, in some of Scotland's finest landscapes.

THE SHARP LITTLE PEAK of Ben A'an, at the eastern end of Loch Katrine, offers wide views in all directions. This one looks to the south-east, over Loch Achray and back to the Lowlands.

Stirling – Key to the Kingdom

As in Edinburgh, Stirling's castle is built on what geologists call a 'crag and tail' – basically, a tough and upstanding rock formation which has resisted the glacier which swept round it. This is the crag part. The movement of the glacier round each side of the resistant rock resulted in a ramp, or tail, of dumped material on the 'downstream' side. Again, like Edinburgh, while the castle clung to the highest point, the original settlement was built on the ramp beyond it. It is likely that Pictish tribes fortified the castle rock and in the Dark Ages there were many tribal groupings in the vicinity: Strathclyde Britons to the south-west, Scots (from Ireland) increasing from the west and Angles to the south.

Thus the important rock was a scene of warfare for centuries until, with a united Scotland, the fortifications became a place where Scottish kings came regularly. In 1124, King David made the community a royal burgh (essentially, a town with trading rights), one of the earliest in Scotland. In those days, the lands to the west of the castle, known as the Carse of Stirling (carse means low-lying ground) were marshy and impassable. Similarly, the slow-flowing, widening river forced routes towards the drier ground near the castle rock. With hills above and below, Stirling's role as a strategic centre was assured.

In the period before the Scots Wars of Independence (1307-14) Stirling Castle was garrisoned by the forces of

THE FORTRESS of Stirling Castle sits on a massive outcrop of basalt. Under the Stewart monarchs the castle became a favoured royal residence and centre of government. Magnificent Renaissance architecture is a feature of the Great Hall and Palace of James V (opposite).

CHURCH OF THE HOLY RUDE With its fine timbered roof, this Gothic church is where John Knox preached and James VI was crowned in 1567.

King Edward I of England, who occupied all of Scotland. The castle was taken back after the Battle of Stirling Bridge in 1297, when the Scots were led by their first freedom-fighter, William Wallace, although it was subsequently retaken and held by English troops until the Battle of Bannockburn in 1314. After the defeat of the English army that day, Scotland's greatest prize and most important fortress was recovered.

Today, there are many significant buildings which show the development of the castle from defensive site to royal residence, and then to a military headquarters. For example, behind the curtain wall and ramparts is the Palace (1538-42) built for King James V. Decorative figures, created by French masons, can be seen on the outside walls. The Great Hall, completed for King James IV in 1503, overlooks the upper courtyard, and in its day has been a seat of the Scottish Parliament, just as the Palace had also housed the Scottish court until the Union of the Crowns in 1603, after which King James VI of Scotland inherited the English crown and went south to London. The long line of Scottish monarchs, known as the royal house of Stewart, is very much associated with Stirling Castle.

The Welsh traveller, Thomas Pennant, toured Scotland in 1769 and his contemporary description varies little from what can be seen today:

'From the top of the castle is by far the finest view in Scotland. To the east is a vast plain rich in corn, adorned with woods, and watered with the River Forth… In this plain is an old abbey, a view of Alloa, Clackmannan, Falkirk, the Firth of Forth and the country as far as Edinburgh. On the north, the Ochil Hills… To the west the strath of Menteith, as fertile as the eastern plain, and terminated by the Highland mountains, among which the summit of Ben Lomond is very conspicuous.'

What has changed since Pennant's day are, firstly, the industrial developments which lie nearer Falkirk to the east and, secondly, the foreground view. From the castle today, the original layout of Stirling can still be appreciated: the historic Old Town lying below the castle, further downhill the Victorian developments including some fine shopping streets, then all of the modern commercial and residential properties typical of a busy Lowland Scottish town, gradually spilling onto the flatlands of the Carse.

There are a number of other early survivors from Stirling's story, notably the Church of the Holy Rude. This has one of Scotland's few remaining medieval vaulted roofs. Tower and nave date partly from around 1456-70. It is the only church in Scotland still in use which witnessed the coronation of a Scottish monarch: that of King James VI in 1567. The adjacent Guildhall was built 1639-49 with funds bequeathed by John Cowane, a wealthy Stirling merchant who funded it for the benefit of less successful merchants or other members of the local trade guilds. Perhaps pride prevented it being a success in that role but much later it became a school and then an epidemic hospital. It is now used for concerts and ceilidhs.

The Old Town of Stirling, centred on Broad Street, still echoes the former life of an old Scottish burgh. Here, for instance, you can see the mercat cross (mercat means market), the symbol of the burgh's commercial life and where important proclamations would have been read. Nearby is the Tolbooth. This handsome building, with its clocktower and gilded weathercock, was the main administrative and legal centre for burgh life and also functioned as the local jail. It dates from 1703. Tenement housing, some of it also dating from the eighteenth century, adds to the ambience, and flanks Broad Street on both sides.

Above Broad Street, winds from the north are checked by the curious façade of a building known as Mar's Wark (work or building). Built in Renaissance style with carved armorial panels and gargoyles, it recalls the Earl of Mar, who, as governor of Stirling

ARGYLL'S LODGING
This is the most impressive 17th-century town house in Scotland. The principal rooms are now restored to their former glory.

portion of its old town wall survives. Look for the most impressive section running uphill from Dumbarton Road, complete with a defence tower or bastion (later used as a gunpowder store). The wall dates from 1547-8. Possibly the best way of exploring this area on foot is to take the Back Walk, built in the late eighteenth century, which runs beside the wall and goes all the way round the castle, offering fine views over the carselands.

Old Stirling Bridge is prominent as seen from the ramparts above. It is the picturesque late fifteenth-century successor to the original wooden Stirling Bridge which played a crucial role in William Wallace's victory over the English occupiers. Wallace held his ragged army back until the heavy armoured knights in the van of the English military had crossed the narrow bridge and unexpectedly found themselves in a marshy meadow. Separated from the rest of the forces and thwarted in their manoeuvres, they were cut down while the rest of the army on the far bank, unable to cross the narrow bridge, looked on. The whole story is told in the National Wallace Monument. This unmistakable tower was built on the Abbey Craig and opened in 1869. Views from the top of the 220 ft (67 m)

STIRLING BRIDGE is thought to have been used by every Scottish sovereign between Robert III and Charles II.

NATIONAL WALLACE MONUMENT (opposite). Built by public subscription, the monument houses an exhibition on Wallace and other Scottish heroes.

Castle, built it in 1570. The structure was badly damaged when the castle was attacked by Bonnie Prince Charlie's Jacobites in the 1745 rebellion. Nearby is Argyll's Lodging, a near-contemporary of Mar's Wark. This is a typical nobleman's town house, now refurbished in period. More atmosphere awaits at the Old Town Jail. This former military detention barracks has likewise been refurbished in period, complete with appropriately costumed and suitably sinister actors.

Aside from the many buildings to visit only moments from the castle in the Old Town, there are a number of other historic features to note. Stirling is unusual amongst Scottish towns in that a considerable

*KING ROBERT I
'The Bruce', renowned
for his victory at
the Battle of
Bannockburn
in 1314.*

tower are superb, although there are 246 steps to reach the viewing platform. Within the halls of the building are displays on the theme of Wallace and his fight for Scotland's freedom, including (at the time of writing) 'a talking head', of the Scots hero.

The scanty remains of Cambuskenneth Abbey lie between the Abbey Craig and the Castle and are conspicuous from high points on both. This was originally an Augustinian settlement, founded by King David I in 1147 and once one of the most important abbeys in Scotland. Many historical events took place here, including, in 1326, the meeting of the first Parliament, with representatives of Scotland's burghs. Today, the site is greatly altered, as much stone was carried away for other buildings in Stirling after the Reformation, so that most of the original abbey exists in little more than floor plan. The Bell Tower or Campanile (originally of 1300) survives, albeit much restored. King James III and his Queen are buried here.

No visitor could say that the site of the Battle of Bannockburn is visually attractive today (in the sense that Killiecrankie or even Culloden are). On a hot midsummer day in 1314, the ancient raised beaches and flood plains of the River Forth, now covered by housing and commercial buildings, were the setting for an engagement between 2500 heavy cavalry, 3000 archers and 15,000 foot soldiers. This was the biggest English army ever to cross the border. Against them stood Scotland's 500 light horsemen, a handful of archers and 5-6000 foot soldiers.

That King Robert the Bruce was victorious on the day owed much to his tactics and leadership, as well as to the local geography of marshy river loops and the preparation of the battlefield with holes and spikes to disable horses. The might of England's armour was rendered ineffective amid the bends of the Bannockburn and the muddy marshes, then skewered on the Scots' long spears. The story is told in detail at the Bannockburn Heritage Centre with its large covered exhibition area and audio-visual. Outside is the Rotunda, a memorial to the battle, and the Borestone, said to have been the command post of the Scottish king.

In the other direction from Bannockburn, looking from the ramparts of the Castle, the long wall of the Ochil Hills tails off at the Dunblane Gap, where road and rail make their way northwards to Perth and the west. Just east of it, the town of Bridge of Allan lies mostly across the south-facing slopes of the Ochils and spills over the plain of the Forth.

Long ago, copper was mined here and a shaft can still be found in the woodlands on the slopes above the town. (The copper was used in the royal mint at Stirling.) A spring which flowed from the vicinity of the shaft was analysed by the owner of the local estate, Sir Robert Abercrombie, around 1820. He was well aware of, firstly, the growing popularity of the Trossachs to the west (thanks to Sir Walter Scott) and, secondly, the fashion for spas and curative water treatments. The analysis was favourable and soon Bridge of Allan had a new life as a fashionable watering place, aided by the arrival of the railway in 1846.

Evidence for this nineteenth-century prosperity can be seen today in the many fine Victorian buildings, including the Holy Trinity Church of 1860 (with Charles Rennie Mackintosh fur-nishings added in 1904); also the Museum Hall with its arcades and Italian palazzo influence. Perhaps its most famous visitors, in retrospect, were the Stevenson family of lighthouse engineers who holidayed here for many years. The novelist Robert Louis Stevenson is associated with a small cave close by the Allan Water, though the cave is actually the start of an uncompleted mineshaft. Local tradition links this cave with Ben Gunn's hideout in Stevenson's children's novel *Treasure Island*. The place is on the Darn Road, an ancient walking route linking Bridge of Allan with the equally venerable Dunblane.

The Celtic missionary St Blane was the founder of Dunblane in the sixth century, his name recalled in this little town (strictly speaking, a city) whose ram-bling narrow streets rise above the Allan Water and are centred on the cathedral. Blane built a church here, though nothing survives, except an early cross-slab and some fragments of sculpture (seen today in the north-west portion of the cathedral choir). A later twelfth-century church was probably demolished to make way for the cathedral founded by Bishop Clement in the early thirteenth century. The earlier church's belltower was incorporated on the south side of the cathedral.

BRIDGE OF ALLAN
This 19th-century spa town is now the home of Stirling University, which was established in 1967. Stuc a' Chroin (centre) and Ben Vorlich (right) are prominent on the horizon.

The building which houses his collection dates from 1688.

Three miles (5 km) east of Dunblane on a windy slope of the Ochil Hills is the battlesite of Sheriffmuir. This was a curious engagement in the Jacobite rebellion of 1715, one of several attempts to return the Stewart monarchy to Britain. The Duke of Argyll, commanding the Clan Campbell, was on the Hanoverian or government side. Hearing that the Jacobites were gathering, he hurriedly took his forces out of Stirling to meet them at Sheriffmuir.

The Earl of Mar, the Jacobite leader, had raised 10,000 men. That day on the hillside they faced only 4000 of the Duke's men; when the two lines clashed the Jacobite-supporting Macdonalds on the right broke through the Campbell militia opposing them. Meanwhile, the left flank of Mar's forces was pushed back by Argyll's cavalry. The day ended in confusion with no decisive result for either side. Next day, with Argyll expecting a fresh attack, he found the Jacobites had instead pulled back to Perth. The battle was over – and so, as it turned out, was the rebellion. Mar had plucked defeat from the jaws of victory. The burial mounds of the slain can still be seen, as can the Gathering Stone, where Argyll is said to have watched the battle.

THE SETTLE INN is on St Mary's Wynd, an ancient route from Stirling to Stirling Bridge.

DUNBLANE CATHEDRAL (opposite). Much of the interior was re-designed by Sir Robert Lorimer and Robert Rowand Anderson.

After the Reformation, Dunblane Cathedral, like so many others, fell into decay, its revenues cut off after local landowners took back the land gifted in earlier times to the church. Dunblane then became a weaving village. The cathedral choir retained its roof and became the parish church. Restoration took place in the late nineteenth century. The setting of the cathedral is made more attractive by some fine domestic architecture of the seventeenth to nineteenth centuries, including the Leighton Library. This is the oldest private library in Scotland and was founded by the Bishop of Dunblane, Robert Leighton (1611-84).

Around the Ochil Hills

From Blairlogie near Stirling the distinctive scarp face of the Ochil Hills runs out eastward towards Dollar for more than 20 miles (32 km). The tough old rocks, ancient lava flows, define the northern edge of the Forth Valley, and meet the softer coal-bearing deposits which slope gently to the widening river: in short, a classic fault line, obvious when looking eastwards from Stirling Castle, or from many points along the valley of the River Forth itself. The long wall of hills, steep to the south, and rolling gently to the north, is unmistakable.

A closer inspection of this line of hills reveals that they are split by steep-sided valleys with fast-flowing burns running out to the south. The hills themselves are grassy rather than heather-covered. It was the nearness of water power and pasture which gave rise to the string of communities along the base of the steep slope. Places like Tillicoultry and Alva originated as mill towns. Originally a cottage-based industry, weaving became a factory process during the first half of the nineteenth century. At that time, the water powered the textile mills, while the sheep which supplied the raw materials grazed on the slopes above. Collectively, these places are known as the 'Hillfoots towns'. The area is still second only to the Scottish Borders in terms of its textile output, though water power is no longer used. Similarly, the raw material of today is not usually local wool, but more likely imported exotic fibres such as cashmere.

Though below the Highland Boundary Fault, the Ochils have an upland character. Their highest point is Ben Cleuch, a big dome whose summit indicator is at

2364 ft (720 m). From it, on a clear day, Goat Fell on the island of Arran to the west can be seen, along with Lochnagar on Deeside in Aberdeenshire, far to the north. Ben Cleuch can be climbed from Tillicoultry or Alva. The Alva starting point is a path east of the town, running above the Silver Burn in the Silver Glen. This deep cleft takes its name from the silver which was formerly mined here. The workings hereabouts date from the early seventeenth century and are said, in 1710, to have earned the Earl of Mar £4000 per week!

Heading east from Stirling, beyond Blairlogie, Menstrie has a castle of the same name: a late sixteenth-century, fortified laird's house (architecturally speaking), restored in 1961 and now boasting a commemorative room to the Baronets of Nova Scotia. The connection is through Sir William Alexander, 1st Earl of Stirling, who was born in Menstrie Castle and encouraged King James VI to found the Order of Baronets of Nova Scotia. Continuing east, Alva is only minutes away, with some notable mill architecture, particularly the former Strude Mill, built around 1820, complete with clock and bellcote to summon the workers. Also in Alva is a Mill Trail Visitor Centre which tells the story of spinning and weaving in the area.

Original equipment can be seen, and the modern mill visited. Alva Glen, immediately behind the town, has attractive waterfalls.

The Ochil Hills Woodland Park is another appealing spot below the high slopes. This was the former policies of Alva House – now demolished – the seat of Sir John Erskine. The sheltered woodlands are open to all, with walkways leading on to Tillicoultry.

Eastwards again, Dollar, with its handsome houses set spaciously back from the Dollar Burn, is noted for its Academy (1820). High above the little town, Castle Campbell sits on a shoulder of the Ochil Hills, with a superb panorama across the Lowlands and the valley of the River Forth. The earliest part of the castle is a relatively simple tower house, dating from the late fifteenth century. This was extended by a south range,

THE MILL TRAIL VISITOR CENTRE in the former mill town of Alva tells the story of spinning and weaving in the old county of Clackmannanshire which is also known as the 'Wee County'. The centre houses some of the original weaving and knitting looms.

then a later east range which includes a highly unusual double-arched arcade (sometimes known as a loggia). This is a feature more often associated with Italianate styles built in sunnier climes – the warm south rather than the cold north. It was added in the late sixteenth century, around the same time as the court-yard was enclosed by a defensive wall. The fortress is associated with the Earls of Argyll, the Chiefs of the Clan Campbell, it being their former principal Lowland seat. Colin Campbell, chief of the Clan Campbell, 1st Earl of Argyll, was appointed Chancellor of Scotland in 1483, and must have made the journey between his castle and the royal court at Stirling many times.

Not far off, the River Devon, flowing out of the Ochils, has cut a deep channel in the soft rocks at Rumbling Bridge. Overhung by ferns and mosses, the river in this mini-gorge most definitely rumbles. The noise is made by boulders tumbling over and over in a deep pot and causing a slightly eerie, deep reverbera-tion. Tourist guides of old (for this was formerly a well-visited tourist spot with its own railway station) called it 'The Devil's Mill'. The excursionists of former times came to picnic and wander the paths on the ferny banks. There is also a curious little bridge, dated 1713, itself spanned by the higher bridge of 1816, which carries the main A823.

Much of the Forth Valley below the Ochils has been worked for coal in earlier days. There are the remains of a beam engine (for pumping out the work-ings) at Sauchie, while Gartmorn Dam near Alloa, though a peaceful, rural spot today, owes its origin to industrial endeavour. The same Earl of Mar who made money from his silver mines, Sir John Erskine (1672-1732), hit upon the idea of using water power to pump out his coal mines on the plain below the hills. The source of this water is today's Gartmorn Dam, set in a tree-fringed and peaceful country park. In its heyday, this artificial loch sent its water down to Alloa to power wool, grain and tobacco mills.

THE OCHIL HILLS present a steep sharp face conspicuous from the Gartmorn Dam Reservoir and much of the Forth Valley.

CASTLE CAMPBELL (opposite). This well preserved stronghold sits high above Dollar.

21

DOUNE CASTLE
A magnificent 14th-century courtyard castle containing a massive frontal block featuring the main buildings which combine tower, gatehouse, hall and kitchen.

The Highland Edge –
Stirling to Callander

It is a short journey from Stirling into the Highlands proper, marked by the sentinel peak of Ben Ledi, but before the visitor even reaches the mountains, there is plenty to see along the edge of the Highland line, and to the south, notably around the outlying Campsie Fells and Fintry Hills.

A few minutes to the west of Stirling, the community of Doune is now chiefly noted for its castle, though in former times the village here was the centre of a pistol-making industry, introduced around 1646. It was also noted for sporran making. This may have a connection

with Doune's role as a cattle-droving centre as it had an important autumn cattle fair. Later, nearby Deanston became noted for cotton spinning, and now houses a well-known distillery.

Many of the buildings around Doune's main street date from the beginning of the nineteenth century, though the mercat cross dates from 1620. Nearby, the Bridge of Teith carries the main A84 road over the River Teith. A bridge was built here in 1535 by one Robert Spittal, apparently to spite the local ferryman who once refused him a crossing. From the bridge there is a fine view downstream to Doune Castle.

Sometimes described as the finest surviving medieval castle in Scotland, this fortress with its 7-ft-(2-m) thick curtain walls remains impressive. It was built by the Regent of Scotland, Robert Stewart, Duke of Albany, in the late fourteenth century. Within the foursquare walls is a courtyard with a main block of buildings, providing great security through its simplicity of layout. An arched passageway with strong gates would have kept intruders at bay, though even if the attackers gained the courtyard, further gates ensured the main buildings could still be held. The lord's hall and retainers' hall even had separate access staircases so that they could be individually defended: all indicative of the turbulent times of medieval Scotland.

From Doune, the main (A84) road to the north-west leads on towards Callander, below the peak of Ben Ledi, with the Trossachs Hills also becoming conspicuous. Callander is typical of the kind of Scottish resort which grew up along the edge of the Highland boundary, a place which for generations has been busy all year round with visitors and day trippers both from far afield and from the populous central belt of Scotland. However, the town predates the tourist boom which began before the end of the eighteenth century. Callander was an old settlement on the military road which led north into the Pass of Leny and then to Lochearnhead and eventually Tyndrum.

Callander took on a new lease of life as a result of the last Jacobite rebellion of 1745. The local land-owners, the Drummonds, were on the losing side and had their lands forfeited, in common with other Jacobite estate owners. The Commissioners of the forfeited estates elected to extend and renew the old village, taking advantage of its sheltered site in a kind of bowl, near the meeting place of the Rivers Teith and Leny. They created the wide main street and simple plan of the town seen today, with its notable focal point the former St Kessog's Church (now the Rob Roy and Trossachs Centre) set in its tree-lined square. Close by are some pleasant riverside walks by the Teith.

On the other side of the busy main street there are some fine woodlands on the slopes behind the town. These are connected by a network of paths and are overlooked by the 890-ft- (271-m) high Callander Crags, a prominent rocky profile rising from the green canopy. There are walking routes to the very top, where there is a Queen Victoria Jubilee Cairn. From here Ben Vorlich and Stuc a' Chroin are the highest hills visible to the north, while the National Wallace Monument and Stirling Castle are conspicuous to the east.

Less energetic visitors should still try to go as far as the Bracklinn Falls, signposted from the main street. The Keltie Water runs in an impressive little gorge here amongst the mixed woodlands of oak, ash and alder. Instead of today's sturdy span, a rickety footbridge formerly stood above the rocky lip over which the water roars. The young Sir Walter Scott is said to have once crossed the bridge on his pony, to win a bet.

Found by turning southwards from the Doune-Callander road, the village of Thornhill runs out along a broad ridge. Once it looked over the undrained marsh-lands of the slow-moving River Forth. Now it is in the centre of one of Scotland's finest hay-making areas, and nearby you can find the Farmlife Centre. In former days, as the marshlands to the south were gradually drained, the village became a gathering-place for artisans, weavers, blacksmiths and agricultural labourers, all dependent on the rich agricultural lands which were developing around them on the very edge of the Highlands.

To see how the area must then have looked it is necessary to journey just a little further west to the

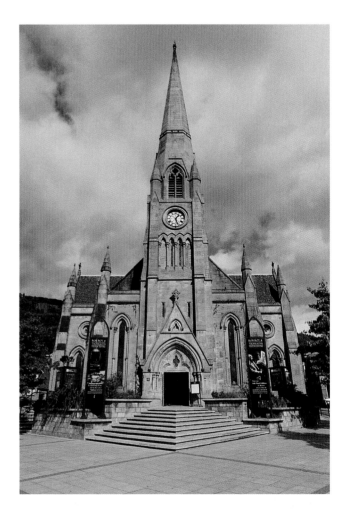

THE ROB ROY & Trossachs Visitor Centre in Callander contains an audio-visual presentation and exhibition on the life of Rob Roy MacGregor.

23

FLANDERS MOSS

Looking south across Flanders Moss, with its birch trees, to the Fintry Hills in the distance. This unique area of the Forth Valley makes up some of the flattest land in Scotland. It contains a type of raised bog which is now an extremely rare form of wildlife habitat in the lowlands.

edge of Flanders Moss. The raised bogs or mosses which have gone from the area around Thornhill are represented by this wet and peaty area, with heather in the drier area and a fringe of birchwoods, still a haven for wildlife. Flanders Moss is the largest surviving raised bog in the UK, even after much reclamation. Most of the Forth Valley was under the sea 8500 years ago. After the sea retreated, there was a gradual change from salt marsh to reed bed and then to bog which became mounded with the volume of accumulated material, hence the term 'raised bog'.

Other villages were built on the higher, drier slopes of the Campsies overlooking the carselands to the south. Kippen, for example, commands a wide view across the carse to the Highland hills. The village grew up on what was the old road between Stirling and Dumbarton, both with important castles. The former burial place of generations of the Earls of Menteith, a church at Kippen is mentioned as early as the thirteenth century, though the gable and bellcote surviving from the Old Kirk of Kippen as seen today date from 1691. In fact, several of the buildings around the Cross, in the village centre, date from the late seventeenth or early eighteenth centuries, including both hotels. Nearby is a traditional smiddy (blacksmith's) in the care of the National Trust for Scotland. Kippen was the scene of a well known skirmish and cattle raid by Rob Roy MacGregor, the noted Highland freebooter.

A high moorland road from Kippen edges the Campsies and drops down to Fintry, strictly speaking, Newton of Fintry, set up as a model village in 1794 by Peter Speirs of Culcreuch Castle, a local mill-owner. He built the development to house his workers and their dwellings are still there on the south side of the main road. Culcreuch Castle is the ancestral home of the Clan Galbraith, and is set in extensive parkland. The castle has a fifteenth/sixteenth-century keep with two later wings. It now functions as a hotel.

A similar development from sleepy village to minor industrial centre occurred in Balfron to the west. The oldest part of this peaceful place below the Campsies is around the church and ancient oak tree (held together by metal bands) by the roadside. Church, inn and a few houses formed the original Clachan of Balfron. (Clachan is related to *clach*, a stone, in Gaelic, and is often the equivalent of kirk-town, in Lowland Scots.) It was formerly on the junction of two drove roads, as routes from both sides of Loch Lomond came together here. Balfron's name is associated with a curious legend about the devouring of the village's children by wolves. It is believed to mean 'the place of sorrow' (Gaelic *bail a bhroin*). The settlement was also of some strategic significance. There are two twelfth/thirteenth-century mottes (earthen mounds, formerly the bases of long-vanished castles of wooden construction) in the vicinity, commanding the routes through the Endrick Valley.

However, the course of Balfron's story was changed when the Ballindalloch Cotton Works were built in 1790 by Robert Dunmore, another landowner with the then fashionable passion for improvement. Soon, houses were built from the riverside mill site up the hill towards the original Clachan. The great mill even provided gas lighting for the village which some describe as the first place in Scotland with this feature. Other improvements included the bridge over the River Endrick, still carrying main road traffic. However, not all the employees were tractable and Balfron even had a spell as a hotbed of Radicalism. Several Balfron weavers took part in the 1820 Radical Uprising and were afterwards forced to emigrate.

Finally, with the closure of the mill before the end

of the nineteenth century and with the arrival of the railway (now also gone), Balfron was well placed within easy reach of Glasgow both for inbound tourists *en route* for the Trossachs and outgoing agricultural supplies, such as milk, to help feed the city folk.

Killearn, even nearer Glasgow, developed in a rough parallel with Balfron. Broadly speaking, the same kind of themes emerge for both places: a cattle-droving staging post (*en route* for the great trysts or cattle sales at Falkirk), weaving with locally grown flax, and basically a farming community within easy reach of the

THE UPLANDS of the Campsies end in the west with the prominent top of Dumgoyne, a landmark for whisky connoisseurs. Below it is the Glengoyne Distillery, noted for its single malt whisky made without peat.

25

THE BROAD TOP of The Whangie reaches a maximum height of 1172 ft (357 m) – more than high enough for an extensive panorama to the north-west where Loch Lomond spills over the boundary of the Highlands and widens out at its shallow southern end.

centres of population in the central belt. Likewise, the railway influenced the role of the little town. In Victorian times Killearn attracted Glasgow business-folk who built their summer residences there. Although the railway has long gone, part of the track-bed is used by the West Highland Way, the official long-distance footpath between Milngavie, on the outskirts of Glasgow, and Fort William.

A short drive south of the town, on the A809, takes the visitor to The Whangie. This is a curious geologi-cal feature, a kind of slightly claustrophobic cleft in a cliff. It can be reached by a short, but fairly steep walk above, and out of sight of the main road. Some geolo-gists say that it was formed by 'glacial plucking'. This means that faces of rock in contact with a glacier become frozen into it and plucked away from the

main cliff. Alternatively, local folklore claims that it was made by the Devil lashing his tail in anticipation as he flew overhead on his way to a meeting with the local witches' coven.

As well as walking above and looking down into the cleft, there is also a path through it. This little expedition starts from very close to The Queen's View (not the only one in Scotland). This one refers to Queen Victoria's first view of Loch Lomond, which she enjoyed in 1879. From here a wide view of the loch is seen, at its southern end where it spreads widely. Beyond, to the north, the hard rocks of the Highland hills confine it to a long narrow channel.

One other place has a strong sense of this Highland edge. The Lake of Menteith is, in geological terms, a very young feature. It was created towards the end of

the last phase of glacier activity in Scotland, about 10,000 years ago, with the melting of an enormous ice-block, the remnant of a glacier grinding out of the mountain masses to the north. Geologists call this kind of loch formation a kettle-hole.

The Lake of Menteith is sometimes described as 'Scotland's only lake' but it is really an early map-maker's error, as the lake part is from Gaelic into Scots as 'laich' meaning a low-lying area. Its chief attraction (other than its angling) is its association with Mary, Queen of Scots. After the defeat of the Scots under the Earl of Arran at the Battle of Pinkie in 1547, the young Mary was taken with her mother, Mary of Guise, to Inchmahome Priory, an Augustinian Priory founded on an island in the loch in 1238 by the 4th Earl of Menteith. (Mary stayed there in safety for three weeks before her journey to France.)

By the end of the same century, the religious community had gone from the island. The ruined priory still survives today, with its spacious church and cloisters. There are traces of a knot garden which is also associated with the young Queen. A ferry runs to the island from the Port of Menteith.

The town of Aberfoyle lies a short way to the west. Though the name is derived from the Gaelic *abar a' phuill* meaning 'the mouth of a muddy pool', the place is usually considered to have no great antiquity. Its setting below the steep pull up to the Trossachs means it has for long attracted tourists. Today it offers a range of visitor attractions, such as The Scottish Wool Centre.

THE LAKE OF MENTEITH
The Augustinian foundation of Inchmahome Priory (below) can be visited by boat in the summer.

27

West & North of Callander – Beyond the Highland Boundary

Within minutes of leaving Callander for the north, the mountains close in. The Pass of Leny makes a grand gateway to the new territory. River and road (and formerly railway) are squeezed together. This has always been an important through route. If you walk the far bank of the River Leny, reaching it by the old railway trackbed (now a walk- and cycle-way), you travel in parts an ancient track which predates the military road from Stirling to Fort William which once ran through here. This road was built in 1750-2 by General Caulfeild. Even then, this was certainly not the earliest military activity here: the Romans built a fort nearby to control the pass.

A little further is the main car park used by walkers climbing Ben Ledi. Though not quite a 'Munro' – a mountain over 3000 ft (914 m) – it is still a hill which, at 2450 ft (750 m), needs respect in poor weather or in snow conditions when the eastern slopes in particular can be treacherous. Ben Ledi is frequently climbed on Midsummer night (when the sun sets in the 'vee' formed between the even higher Ben More and Stob Binnein to the north-west). For the old Celtic peoples, however, this was a less important occasion than May Day (traditionally called Beltane), which was associated with practices involving the kindling of hilltop fires and also sacrifices: rituals which go back to pre-Christian times. The habit of climbing Ben Ledi on Midsummer night is probably a continuous folk memory, with the two dates perhaps becoming confused. Certainly, Ben Ledi is not the only Scottish hill with a well-worn path to its summit that is especially busy on both May Day and Midsummer.

From the Ben Ledi car park it is easy to continue on foot or by bike all the way to Strathyre on the quieter west bank of Loch Lubnaig. Just where the Pass of Leny opens out at the south end of the Loch is the ancient St Bride's Chapel, whose tiny burial place is associated with the branch of the Mackinlays related to the US President of the same name. The main road takes the east shore and offers fine views of the craggy shoulders between Ben Ledi and Ben Vane to the north. Further north, on the east side, a right of way goes due north into Glen Ample, once a hunting forest of the Scottish monarchs. This is a popular route not just for low-level walkers but also for hillwalkers setting out for a day on Stuc a' Chroin or Ben Vorlich (two Munros which are prominent on the approaches to Callander).

Beyond the top end of Loch Lubnaig, Strathyre must formerly have been the first real Highland settlement encountered by early tourists. Dorothy Wordsworth was very complimentary about it in her diary during her visit of 1803, describing it as a 'very sweet valley', and the place won further fame with the once popular and much-parodied ballad *Bonnie Strathyre*, by Sir Harold Boulton:

> *Till the peak of Ben Vorlich is girdled with fire,*
> *And the evening falls gently on Bonnie Strathyre.*

Upper Strathyre, with its fertile riverside fields, was also an important droving stance in former days, where the cattle could graze on their southward trek.

BEN LEDI (opposite) lies right on the edge of the Highlands and is a conspicuous landmark not just from Callander's main street, but also from many parts of the eastern lowlands, including the ramparts of Edinburgh Castle.

29

Beyond Strathyre, Balquhidder Glen also runs off to the west. Though sometimes overlooked in the dash to the north and west, this cul-de-sac road is well worth exploring. When the Highland clans ruled beyond the Highland boundary, this was quite an important place, with a much higher population, thanks partly to the space for farming, especially by the river, and because the glen was on a natural crossing place. Formerly important hill routes come in from Brig o' Turk and the Trossachs via Glen Buckie, and from Glen Dochart over Kirton Glen behind the church. Dorothy and William Wordsworth passed this way, with Dorothy noting:

LOCH VOIL, in Gaelic loch a'bheothuil *– loch of the quick running flood – refers to the flood-prone River Balvaig which flows from its eastern end.*

As a kind of drove road service station, the place also acquired a reputation through its numerous alehouses. Eventually, Strathyre also provided labour for the forestry that grew up all around it, especially in the post-war years, by which time much of the original broad-leaved cover had been replaced by extensive conifer plantations. For explorers on foot, there is the railway trackbed walk, and an attractive side road which runs round to Balquhidder. To admire the setting of the village in its glen, there is also a forestry track to a rewarding viewpoint, Beinn an t-Sithein, (Gaelic for the fairy hill) above Strathyre to the west.

'At the end of Loch Voil the vale is wide and populous – large pastures with many cattle, large tracts of corn.'

Balquhidder formerly had its own annual fair, dedicated to St Angus, and held on the river flats nearby. Highlanders came from miles around. In olden days this was the country of the Maclarens. The MacGregors also claimed territory here, much of it later confiscated by King James IV.

The ruinous Balquhidder Kirk dates from 1631 and was built on the site of a pre-Reformation chapel, once visited by King James IV. The church is said to have had a congregation of 600, in the glen's densely populated days. The 'new' Parish Church dates from 1853, and its bell predates it, having been bought for the earlier building by its most famous minister, the Reverend Robert Kirk (1644-92). He was later to achieve a certain notoriety when he was appointed to Aberfoyle. There he was said to have communicated with the fairy world and was eventually spirited away. His book *The Secret Commonwealth of Elves, Fauns and Fairies* relates much about the world of the little people in an eerily matter-of-fact kind of way.

Near the present church are a couple of worthwhile walks. A fairly steep path goes north up to Creag an Tuirc, the rallying ground of the Maclarens (who formerly held the glen). There is a magnificent view of the length of the glen, with Loch Voil stretching out towards the shoulders of the big hills which lie to the west. This path comes off the main route up Kirkton Glen, through the mature (and partly felled) plantations. The track up Kirkton Glen is worth exploring for the upland scenery above and beyond the dense plantings. There is a beautiful little hill loch to enjoy, sandpiper-haunted and crystal clear. This is Lochan an Eireannaich (literally 'little loch of the Irishman'), while further on, up by the watershed at the head of the glen, are some good spots if you are interested in alpine plants. Listen out for ring ouzels singing, in late spring and summer.

This route would certainly have been known to Rob Roy MacGregor. Back down in Balquhidder Glen, his grave is by the church, re-using a fourteenth-century horizontal gravestone (old, even in Rob's day), and is a popular excursion. There are other

MacGregor connections further up the glen, beyond Loch Voil. The site of his house is at the road end by Inverlochlarig. This is the starting point for a number of high-level walks, including the conquest of Stob Binnein and Ben More, the high and handsome twins best seen from Glen Dochart to the north. During the Wordsworths' expedition, they noted the increasingly fertile look of the valley from this point back eastward. Their visit was in September and the harvest was in full swing. One of the harvesters, a pretty Highland girl, inspired the famous poem *The Solitary Reaper*, with its haunting lines:

> *No sweeter voice was ever heard*
> *In spring-time from the cuckoo-bird*

ROB ROY'S GRAVE is still a place of pilgrimage for tourists today. Though active in Jacobite affairs, and proclaimed an outlaw for many years, Rob Roy was able to return to his homelands, and died peacefully in his bed in 1734.

GLEN OGLE, looking south towards Lochearnhead. In the distance the prominent peaks of Ben Vorlich and Stuc a'Chroin (hill of the bay and peak of harm or danger) are popular with hill walkers from central Scotland.

> *Breaking the silence of the seas*
> *Among the farthest Hebrides.*

The weaver poet Robert Tannahill (1776-1810) was also inspired hereabouts, composing the original version of what eventually became the popular song *The Wild Mountain Thyme*, a standard in many a folk-singer's repertoire at clubs and ceilidhs. Tannahill's original version is placed specifically in the local braes:

> *Let us go, lassie, go*
> *To the Braes o' Balquhither*
> *Where the blaeberries grow*
> *Mang the bonny Highland heather.*

Meanwhile, the main road runs by Kingshouse, not the only one in Scotland, as the name recalls the military road, with its inns at regular intervals. Lochearnhead is only a few minutes away to the north. A natural junction with roads from Perth in the east, the loch and hence the settlement may have got its name from Eireann, Ireland, referring to early Christian missionaries from Ireland. (It also curiously echoes Lochan an Eirannaich in nearby Kirkton Glen.)

Like Balquhidder and Strathyre to the south, Lochearnhead in the past was bound up with crofting and cattle-droving. As a major water-sports centre, it is still popular with visitors. Its development as a tourism centre was originally helped by the railways which used to come in from the north and west. The end-on view of Loch Earn from high above Lochearnhead was sometimes described as the finest view from any railway carriage in Britain. This section of line closed in 1965, though the trackbed from Lochearnhead to the head of Glen Ogle is now in use as a walkway – so the view can still be appreciated.

The road up Glen Ogle brings an increasingly wild air to the landscape. Some of the tumbled rocks on the western slopes fell in the 1960s and hastened the closure of the railway whose trackbed clings to the western slopes. This is the glen described famously by Queen Victoria in her diary of 10 September 1842 as 'a sort of long pass, putting one in mind of prints of the Kyber Pass' – to which it has been compared ever since.

Queen Victoria came south and down Glen Ogle in her carriage, hence may even have missed the fine panorama of peaks behind her – the distinct profile of the mountains behind Killin to the north-east, notably the lumpy ridge of Meall nan Tarmachan and the high ground of Ben Lawers. Both are noted for their alpine plants. Strictly speaking this is now Breadalbane, a swathe of land from Loch Tay to Tyndrum, which translates from the Gaelic *braighe albann* as 'the high grounds of Scotland'.

The main road drops to the curiously named Lix Toll, which some believe to be originally named after a Roman milestone for 59, though it might also be from *leac*, a Gaelic word meaning a slab or flagstone. To the west is the attractive village of Killin, noted for the Falls of Dochart.

These falls would be worth travelling to see wherever they were located but for the less adventurous traveller it is a bonus that they lie close to a place with hotels, shops, restaurants and all the trappings of a small Highland resort. Killin is a very old settlement associated with legends of Fingal, a Celtic hero. Some say the place name actually means Cill Fhinn – the burial place of Fingal. Equally plausibly, it could mean simply the church by the linn, another Scottish word meaning a waterfall or rocky narrowing.

Among the clans associated with the area is the Clan MacNab, descendants of the Abbots of Glendochart. (Both lay and clerical abbots in the Celtic church were allowed to marry, so that MacNab is literally Mac an Aba, or children of the abbot.) The clan burial ground is on the island of Inchbuie, just downstream of the bridge at the lower end of the Falls of Dochart. The MacNabs were eclipsed by the mighty Clan Campbell who gradually took over their lands.

The Breadalbane headquarters of the Campbells was formerly Finlarig Castle, a neglected ruin (with a decidedly sinister atmosphere) surrounded by dark and

THE FALLS OF DOCHART, Killin, run into nearby Loch Tay. The bridge over the falls, which was built in 1760, is a popular viewpoint.

MOIRLANICH LONGHOUSE, close to Killin in Glen Lochay. This longhouse is an outstanding example of a traditional cruck-frame cottage and byre dating from the mid 19th century.

BEN CHALLUM, from the east (opposite). Gaelic: Malcolm's hill, at 3362 ft (1025 m) it dominates the head of Glen Lochay.

ancient Healing Stones of St Fillan have pride of place on permanent display – just one element in the life and legends of the area interpreted in the Centre.

Glen Lochay is reached from Killin by way of a narrow cul-de-sac road which starts just before the main road bridge over the River Lochay, and makes an especially scenic and attractive excursion. There are signs of ancient settlement within the glen, including

sombre trees to the east of the village and reached by the bridge across the Dochart. This sixteenth-century fortress was built by Sir Duncan Campbell, second laird of Glenorchy. One of his descendants, known as Black Duncan of the Cowl, achieved notoriety for his methods of dealing out justice on behalf of King James VI, which seem to have frequently involved the beheading pit, which survives just beyond the walls of Finlarig.

As well as the ruinous Finlarig and the Falls of Dochart, visitors usually take in the Breadalbane Folklore Centre. St Fillan, an Irish missionary who was active in this area, is associated with healing stones. Remarkably, these eight relics of the Saint have survived. They were for long preserved in the mill close by the Dochart Bridge, lying in a bed of straw which was renewed every Christmas. With the conversion of this building into the Breadalbane Folklore Centre, the

cup- and ring-marked stones, as well as traces of a prehistoric village. However, the most easily found place is only a mile (1.6 km) north-west of Killin. Hard by the road side, the Moirlanich Longhouse is an outstanding example of a nineteenth-century cruck-framed cottage and byre and has been recently restored by the National Trust for Scotland. It contains particularly fine examples of box beds and a 'hingin lum' over the main cooking range. The adjacent museum explains the story of the restoration of the longhouse and the daily lives of its previous inhabitants.

East of Killin, the main road running along the north shore of Loch Tay is joined by a narrow road which runs over a high pass and drops to Glen Lyon. High on this road, the National Trust for Scotland built a visitor centre which interprets the flora of Ben Lawers, Perthshire's highest mountain.

The Trossachs

Arguably the Trossachs, along with Loch Lomond, are the most famous part of Scotland, in scenic terms. How this came about is related to the story of tourism in Scotland and how the very concept of a 'tourist' came about. Ultimately two factors about the Trossachs are important. Firstly, they are located within easy reach of the populated central belt of Scotland and, secondly, though their hills and lochs are wild and grand, they were not too grand or terrifying for those early tourists who really felt they were on a daring expedition to unexplored territory.

The Trossachs became the very byword for Scottish scenery, yet have both a vague definition of where exactly the area starts and stops and also exactly what the word means. Dorothy Wordsworth, just one of many early travellers here, records in her *Journal* of 1803 (*Recollections of a Tour Made in Scotland*): 'I believe the word Trossachs signifies "many hills": it is a name given to all the eminences at the foot of Loch Ketterine (sic), and about half a mile beyond.' Dorothy, it seems, was given wrong information in the translation.

The Rev. Patrick Graham, minister at Aberfoyle, was another early authority who had a stab at defining the word Trossachs (then spelt 'Trosachs' by contemporary writers such as Sir Walter Scott). He wrote in his *Sketches of Perthshire*, published in 1806, that the word meant 'the rough or bristled territory'. Though he gave no etymology or any other explanation as to why he came to that conclusion, the definition subsequently satisfied generations of other guidebook writers who cheerfully repeated it.

Yet another explanation has since been offered and frequently appears in print. Trossachs is really *trasdaichean* or *trosaichean*, which is an obsolete Gaelic word used in the plural and meaning a transverse glen which joins two others. The only snag here is that the very heart of where the Trossachs are supposed to lie, which is somewhere in the rough country between Loch Katrine and Loch Achray – barely a mile apart – can hardly be described as a transverse glen.

As to defining them in a geographical sense, it is likely that though a whole generation of earlier nineteenth-century writers were content with Trossachs lying around Loch Katrine, later publicity material produced by the railway companies (mostly the North British) who ran a popular Trossachs and Loch Lomond tour, widened the definition of the area to take in all of the country between Ben Ledi, near Callander, and Loch Lomond itself. If broadening the area in an east-west axis, it then seems a short step to include Loch Ard and Loch Chon, with Aberfoyle as a southern gateway, and to extend northwards up to the edge of Balquhidder. This is the Trossachs in the broadest sense!

If their definition in geography and etymology is debatable, what is beyond dispute is that they achieved their status as the byword for Scottish scenery extremely early on in the story of tourism in Scotland. The eighteenth century was, broadly speaking, a time of advancement, when minds were set towards order and harmony, for example, in landscape. It was during this time that some of the finest gardens around stately homes were laid out; nature was tamed, reflecting the order and symmetry of the neo-classical architecture.

THE VIEW FROM BEN A'AN to the higher Ben Venue to the south-west (opposite), spans the very heart of the Trossachs. Hidden in trees is the former pathway which once ran between Loch Achray westward to the larger Loch Katrine, now a twisting road to the car park by the shore of Loch Katrine.

these early tourists eager for a brush with landscape which was wild and in disorder. The Cult of the Picturesque was in place before the beginning of the nineteenth century.

So it came about that in 1790, the Rev. Dr James Robertson, minister of Callander, made his contribution to the *Statistical Account of Scotland* (published in 1794) and was able to devote several pages to a theme which he was able to entitle 'Romantic Prospects' – clearly a concept which his readership already understood. He started his piece with the sentence: 'The Trossachs are often

LOCH KATRINE
This attractive loch may take its name from the Welsh cethern *meaning 'furies', although Sir Walter Scott derived the name from the 'caterans' who were free-booters found in this area in former times.*

Civilisation, it would have been widely assumed, most certainly stopped at the Highland line. Those north of it were rebels and savages.

Inevitably, there was a counter reaction and the age of the Romantics came about. The wild and uncouth Highlander became the 'noble savage'. People began to view the Highlands in a different light. Inevitably, the harmony of hill, loch and wooded crag known as the Trossachs commanded attention not just because it was suitably wild and romantic but also because it was the first part of the Highlands encountered by many of

visited by persons of taste, who are desirous of seeing nature in her rudest and most unpolished state'. He goes on to describe the late eighteenth-century equivalent of what today would be called 'tourism infrastructure': 'The Hon. Mrs Drummond of Perth has erected booths of wicker work, in the most convenient places, for the accommodation of strangers, who visit this wild and picturesque landscape; and the tenants of the next farm are very ready to show the beauties of the place to travellers'. These sound like the ancestors of tourist information centres and bed-and-breakfast establishments.

The first 'modern' account of the Trossachs as a place suitable for 'persons of taste' to visit was a travelogue entitled *A Companion, and useful guide to the beauties of Scotland, to the Lakes of Westmoreland, Cumberland, and Lancashire… to which is added, a more particular Description of Scotland, especially that part of it called the Highlands.*

The intrepid author was the Hon. Mrs Murray of Kensington (as she styled herself). She arrived in the Trossachs in the autumn of 1796, already familiar with the 1794 *Statistical Account.* She was fully equipped with carriage and servants, a travelling wine cupboard and larder and a firm determination to penetrate the wilderness. Her entourage left Callander and nearly got her coach as far as Loch Katrine. Proceeding boldly on foot, she found woodcutters at work by its shores, so she asked them to row her around the loch. Her description of the excursion includes an early mention of the mountainous hollow on the south side of Loch Katrine, not far from the Trossachs pier, which is now marked on maps as Coire nan Uruisgean or the Goblins' Cave.

This name was made famous by Sir Walter Scott. The woodmen who showed Mrs Murray around referred to it as the 'Den of the Ghost', suggesting that even then it had an eerie reputation among the locals. She also described the beautiful wooded islands, related how her coach almost turned over in a ford at Glen Finglas, and how her all-day expedition was almost benighted before reaching Callander. Even then her adventure was not over. Agriculture in those days still had priority over tourism. Mrs Murray returned to her inn to discover that the carpets in

THE BANKS OF LOCH KATRINE are kept unspoilt and free from harmful developments because of its status as a water supply for Glasgow. The north shore pictured here has a road used only by waterworks maintenance vehicles, walkers and cyclists.

her room had been removed to cover hayricks from the rain!

Her published volume doubtless inspired others to visit. In 1803, the Wordsworths, William and his sister Dorothy, arrived, along with the poet Samuel Coleridge. They had certainly heard of The Trossachs and, having been given directions from a serving girl in the inn at Luss on Loch Lomond, they crossed that loch, landed at Inversnaid and made their way down to Loch Katrine. After an overnight stay at Glengyle, at the west end of the loch, they travelled eastwards. On the way, William stopped at the old graveyard at Portnellan, still to be seen today. He had been told that this was the resting place of Rob Roy MacGregor, the Highland Robin Hood. His poem *Rob Roy's Grave* followed on from this visit. However, his hostess of the previous evening had misinformed him and, as any visitor knows today, the famous MacGregor is buried at Balquhidder.

The Wordsworths were rowed the length of the loch (while Coleridge walked), Dorothy, like Mrs Murray before her, remarking on the Den of the Ghost (the Goblins' Cave). Similarly, they reached the huts built for shelter near the Loch Katrine end of the Trossachs defile. There they found Coleridge waiting. Dorothy recorded how he 'hailed as with a shout of triumph from the door of one of them, exulting in the glory of Scotland'. Though it seemed to have rained a great deal, these Romantics found the Trossachs much to their taste for their picturesque wildness, and returned west to Loch Lomond well pleased with their adventure.

Seven years later, there burst upon the literary scene

LOCH CHON (opposite), by the road to Stronachlachar and Inversnaid, offers pleasant sheltered walking on its west bank, the route also taken by the Loch Katrine aqueduct.

the work which would make the name of the Trossachs known throughout the literary world. *The Lady of the Lake*, in form a dramatic verse narrative, is more or less neglected today, but was a literary sensation when published in 1810. Sir Walter Scott already had a knowledge of the Trossachs' topography. As a law apprentice he had had to serve a writ on some difficult tenants in Balquhidder, to the north, around 1790. Later, as a qualified lawyer in 1793, he received several invitations from well-to-do legal friends, several of whom had properties along the Highland edge. One of these was Cambusmore, near Callander.

At the same time he was already achieving literary fame as the author of *The Lay of the Last Minstrel* and *Marmion*. After he had conceived the idea for *The Lady of the Lake* he used Cambusmore as a base for research – even checking out travelling times between places mentioned in the poem in order to make the tale plausible. The poem was published in the spring of 1810, and, after early sales of 20,000 copies, the first waves of inspired visitors began to explore the topography of the Trossachs that Scott had described. As Alexander Cadell, one of Scott's literary colleagues, later told his biographer, Lockhart: 'The whole country rang with praise of the poet; crowds set off to view the scenery of Loch Katrine… and as the book came out just before the season for excursions, every house and inn in that neighbourhood was crammed with a constant succession of visitors.'

The narrative part of the poem is set in the time of King James V and concerns the outcome of a stag hunt. The pursued stag is trailed to the heart of the Trossachs by the hero Fitz-James, who meets Ellen

whose name is recalled in Ellen's Isle, still marked on maps today. (The heroine lived in a 'sylvan hall' on a wooded island on the loch.) Other romantic elements include the raising of the fiery cross to call the local clans to arms, rival suitors for the hand of Ellen, and a king in disguise. (There is even a character called Brian the Hermit!) The appeal for its first readers was the way that the narrative was so firmly grounded in the landscape. Book in hand, the avid romantic could identify hilltop and crag:

High on the south, huge Ben Venue
Down on the lake in masses threw
Crags, knolls, and mounds,
*   confusedly hurled*
The fragments of an earlier world.

By the time of Scott's death in 1832, the romantic cult centred on the Trossachs had grown to the extent that the new owners of the Drummond estates around Loch Katrine went as far as building a replica of the 'sylvan hall' on Ellen's Isle. Its centre-piece was a living tree and its Gothic windows were likewise formed of natural branches. There were heather couches and wild animal hides hung from the walls. It was burned to the ground by vandals around 1836.

Another early development was the arrival of an eight-oared galley, the *Water Witch*, manned by sturdy costumed Highlanders, who monopolised the traffic for several years. These same Highlanders were to come under suspicion in 1843 when the first steamer, a small iron boat called *Gipsy*, mysteriously sank at her moorings a week after she had been laboriously dragged to the loch by her owners, eager to capitalise on the tourist traffic. The indirect successor to the first steamboat is today's SS *Sir Walter Scott*, which has sailed on the loch for almost a century.

With the age of steam came the railways to continue the popularity of the area. The area's official guide, published by the North British Railway in 1914,

SS SIR WALTER SCOTT, a coal-fired steamer, built in 1900, runs cruises on Loch Katrine in summer.

FACTOR'S ISLAND on Loch Katrine (opposite), recalls the Duke of Montrose's estate manager, held captive here by Rob Roy.

ROB ROY MACGREGOR was born hereabouts at Glengyle in 1671, at the now less frequented western end of Loch Katrine.

modestly declaims that 'To the tourist who undertakes the journey no surfeit of laudation is possible, for in The Trossachs the superlative reigns absolute' – which seems to mean that visitors were going to see the finest scenery anywhere in the known world.

Both Aberfoyle and Callander are without rails today, but the coal-fired *Sir Walter Scott* still takes its pleasure cruisers out past Ellen's Isle today. If this seems an anachronism, then at least it is rated as a low pollution risk – very necessary, as Loch Katrine is Glasgow's water supply. The pure water of the loch is taken by pipe and aqueduct 27 miles (43 km) to Mugdock Reservoir on the outskirts of Glasgow.

For its day (1855-9), the Loch Katrine aqueduct was a massive undertaking which involved tunnelling through the rounded ridge separating Loch Katrine from the glen to the south in which Loch Chon sits. Tough rock and wild country made progress slow. Walkers today taking the attractive path along the west side of Loch Chon can follow this pipe-track, with its odd hollow stone pillars (really ventilation shafts) rising at intervals out of the greenery. There are also stone aqueducts at various points on the route, now mellowed and moss-grown, yet still carrying out their function long after the armies of navvies who built them have gone. The sluices where the water leaves Loch Katrine are at a building called Royal Cottage, recalling Queen Victoria's official opening of the works on a day, appropriately, of pouring rain in 1859. It is also possible (on foot) to trace the ventilation shafts up the hill from this point, dropping down to the Inversnaid road just north-west of Loch Chon.

No visitor can wander through the Trossachs for long without encountering Rob Roy MacGregor. His name has even been borrowed by the Rob Roy and Trossachs Visitor Centre in Callander, the main Trossachs orientation point. However, Rob Roy was famous in the Trossachs long before – in fact, he was, without exaggeration, a 'legend in his own lifetime', long before Hollywood got hold of the story.

He was born in 1671 at Glengyle at the now less frequented western end of Loch Katrine. In those days, it was a much more populated place, as the glen itself was on a main drove route from Loch Lomond and the west. Cattle were to play a major part in Rob's life, likewise the prevailing politics of the time. Rob lived through most of the period when the Jacobites were active. Supporters of the exiled King James, they were determined to oust the House of Hanover and return the Stuart monarchy. His story has now become much better known, thanks to books and a film, but it was probably Sir Walter Scott who portrayed him in his essence: as a symbol of a proud and independent Highland way of life that had no place as the dominating (and civilising?) forces of the Lowlands took over.

Rob operated just over the Highland line as a cattle dealer, drover and thief. The Trossachs were his home territory, recalled in place names such as Factor's Island on Loch Katrine, where he once held hostage the estate factor of the Duke of Montrose (his arch-enemy). He would have been familiar with the old drove road along Loch Katrine and the shelter afforded by Coire nan Uruisgean if 'lifted' (i.e. stolen) herds had to be kept out of sight. Likewise, he would have known the now unfrequented hill paths which lead north to Balquhidder and his later home.

Rob's old haunts are mostly deserted now. It is a curious characteristic of the Trossachs' landscapes as enjoyed by visitors today that they mop up and absorb their temporary population so that it is perfectly possible still to find some peaceful parts. Visitors come to the Trossachs for much the same reasons as they always did, though over the years there have been many changes. The Duke's Road, for example, which snakes up from Aberfoyle and crosses the forested rough ground before dropping to the heart of the Trossachs, recalls the Duke of Montrose. He originally built it because of the popularity of the Trossachs but it took on its modern form as recently as 1932.

A VIEW from the very heart of the Trossachs, where the Duke's Road, between Aberfoyle and the glen leading in to Loch Katrine, reaches its highest point. Ben A'an is the peak on the right horizon, with Loch Katrine in the centre of the picture.

The once extensive oakwoods, whose bark was harvested to be used in the tanning industry, have mostly gone from the slopes of Ben Venue. State forestry has been practised here since the 1920s. This acquisition of unprofitable land of high scenic value has resulted in extensive coniferous plantings now approaching maturity. These are mostly of sitka and Norway spruce, with some Scots pine – the only native species – and lodgepole pine on drier slopes.

Much of the Trossachs lies within the Queen Elizabeth Forest Park, which was established in 1953. The park has its own visitor centre above Aberfoyle and from here, like the rest of the area, a well established network of walkers' trails makes its way through the dense woodlands. Further along the Duke's Road, just to the west of the end of Loch Drunkie, there is a viewpoint above the main road where the main Trossachs hills can be made out rising above the blanket of conifers. An indicator helps identify the peaks in view. This was the point from where the nineteenth-century poet Henry Chauncey Townshend looked out after he and his companions had walked up from the Aberfoyle side. He saw 'Half the horizon… filled with mountains, tossed and tumbled about like an ocean arrested in its wildest rage' – according to a *Descriptive Tour in Scotland*, published in 1840. (Perhaps Romantic Poets tended to exaggerate a lot.)

A footpath goes downhill from here into the woodlands to emerge at Brig o' Turk, a small community moments to the east of Loch Achray. The name is from Gaelic *tuirc*, meaning a wild boar, extinct since the sixteenth century. From here it is possible to go north along a good road to discover the often over-looked Glen Finglas, part of the water supply complex and now dammed to feed into Loch Katrine – hence the motorable road as far as the waterworks. There were formerly impressive falls here, now tamed by the works and, in typical Trossachs fashion, there is also a tale of romance. This time, however, it does not have Sir Walter Scott creating fiction but instead the sad tale of the critic John Ruskin. He came here with his wife Euphemia Gray and his friend the painter John Millais. With his canvas set up in a tent in the glen, the painter worked on a portrait of the critic in the dramatic wooded setting. Perhaps the stern Ruskin was thinking too much on his latest work, *Lectures on Architecture and Painting*, which he was then writing. Whatever the reason, the romance of the place obviously affected Euphemia. There in the glen she fell in love with Millais and within a year, scandalising the literary establishment, her marriage was annulled and she settled down with the painter.

Romance, dramatic scenery, hills and woods which swallow up visitors galore – nowhere else is quite like the Trossachs – and all within easy reach of some of the most densely populated parts of Scotland. Small wonder Callander's main street is busy all year round. There is a sense of amused frustration in the words of the journalist HV Morton in his classic work *In Search of Scotland* when he writes how a writer can travel and hunt for months looking for the real Scotland. In doing so, he finds himself 'enduring heat, cold, fatigue, high teas, Sabbaths, kirks, and at the end comes suddenly on the whole thing in concentrated form, boiled down to the very essence – in the Trossachs'.

LOCH ACHRAY (opposite), provides a suitable sylvan setting for the former Trossachs Hotel, whose Victorian builders were inspired by Sir Walter Scott's brand of Romanticism.

Around Loch Lomond

Loch Lomond is the largest loch in Scotland in terms of its surface area. Until very recent geological times – the last Ice Age, about 10,000 years ago – Loch Lomond was an arm of the sea, like its near neighbour Loch Long today. Around that time, what geologists call the Loch Lomond re-advance glacier came grinding southwards down the deep trench of the loch and dumped its ground-off material to form a dam around Balloch at the south end of today's loch. Loch Lomond was formed behind this glacial debris, a mere 27 ft (8 m) above sea level – almost a fjord. Instead, it is linked to the sea by the short River Leven, running down the industrialised Vale of Leven.

If the Loch Lomond approaches from the south do not feel at all Highland it is because they are not. The Highland Boundary Fault still lies to the north. Loch Lomond is really two lochs in one. The southerly portion is wide and shallow – here the glacier was able to spread out over the soft Lowland sandstones. The lochside has pleasant leafy lanes, cultivated fields and woods. To the north, it is very different, with the narrow loch confined by the slates and schists of mountainous shoulders on both sides – truly Highland.

One of the best places to appreciate this is from the top of the little Duncryne Hill, immediately behind the village of Gartocharn. Duncryne is the core or vent of an ancient volcano, one of several humps poking through the local sandstones. For all its 470 ft (142 m) it gives a view quite out of proportion to its size. Noticeable in the middle distance is a line of islands, from Inchmurrin to Inchcailloch, which trace the line of the Boundary Fault as it runs down from the lumpy top of Conic Hill further to the east. This hill behind Balmaha is another fine viewpoint, lying on the West Highland Way, but it takes a little more effort to reach the top.

Drymen is another usual approach to the loch from the south. Taking its name from Gaelic *druim*, a ridge, the community grew around what was formerly the lowest bridging point of the River Endrick. Situated in good farming land, it used to hold a notable cattle market and fair, and still has an important annual agricultural show. The community was also on the important military road which once linked Stirling and Dumbarton Castles. Today's main road is still carried over the River Endrick on a handsome five-arched bridge, which was built by the military road builder, General Caulfeild, in 1765.

The lands around Drymen and northwards on Loch Lomondside are associated with the Dukes of Montrose, who acquired them from the Buchanans in the seventeenth century. The seat of the Dukes of Montrose, the original Buchanan House, close to the River Endrick, was destroyed by fire in 1850. Its successor, Buchanan Castle, had a chequered career including a spell as a military hospital when its most famous occupant was Rudolph Hess, Hitler's deputy, who crash-landed his plane on his peace-making mission. The

north, at Craigrostan. The Pass of Balmaha was considered important enough as a Highland gateway that during the 1715 Jacobite rebellion, for example, the Duke of Argyll kept a garrison at Drymen to watch over it.

Conic Hill marks the place where the West Highland Way drops down to the loch as well. This popular 'official' long-distance waymarked footpath runs 95 miles (152 km) from the outskirts of Glasgow to Fort William. With its jetties and boat-yard, Balmaha is the starting point for island ferries and cruises and it is easy to

THE RIVER ENDRICK, fed by the waters from the Campsies and the Fintry Hills, runs slowly through marsh-lands at the south end of Loch Lomond, part of a Scottish Natural Heritage (SNH) National Nature Reserve.

roofless building (private) can be seen in the view north-westwards towards Loch Lomond from the little park opposite the Buchanan Arms Hotel in Drymen. (Go through the gate and up the slope.)

Drymen is the gateway to the east bank cul-de-sac road by Loch Lomond. This attractive and popular route reaches the lochside at Balmaha. The original Pass of Balmaha is higher into the hills to the east. This was the route often used in cattle droving, legitimate or otherwise, especially in the days of Rob Roy (again) as he, before being outlawed, held lands to the

reach, for example, Inchcailloch from here. This translates from the Gaelic as 'the island of the (old) women', a reference to the religious settlement founded here in the seventh century by St Kentigerna, mother of St Fillan. A thirteenth-century church survives and for generations this was the most sacred burial place for the local clansmen (including one of Rob Roy's ancestors). The island is a nature reserve in the care of Scottish Natural Heritage, with a 2-mile (3-km) walk through the island's oak woods and a wonderful view northwards from the highest point on the island.

Inchcailloch is just one of about 33 islands in the loch, from the substantial down to the little chips of greenery such as Island I Vow. This little place once had a tiny hermitage and chapel on it and it is said that an early-flowering daffodil variety grows there, possibly cultivated by the priests for decorating the chapel for Easter festivities. Wordsworth made the island the setting for his poems *The Brownie* and *The Brownie's Cell*. Most of the islands, notably the larger ones, are at the southern end of the loch, though Island I Vow is one of the exceptions, rising out of the loch in its narrower northern portion which is around 600 ft (183 m) above sea level.

There is also an ancient jingle concerning the loch which talks of 'a wave without a wind, a fish without a fin, and a floating island' – the meaning of which has never been satisfactorily explained. The islands have long had a history as places of defence. The Earls of Lennox had a stronghold on Inchmurren from at least the fifteenth century. The Macfarlane chiefs had defensive bases on the island of Inveruglas and on Eilean Vou, while the Galbraiths built on the tiny islet south of Inchtavannach, which still bears the name Inchgalbraith. A picturesque ruin survives here today.

Meanwhile, little Clairinch, south of Inchcailloch, is said to have been the first landholding of the local Buchanans, and gave the clan their battle-cry. The more substantial Inchlonaig, off Luss to the north, is associated with Robert the Bruce. Its yew trees were originally said to have been planted on his instructions, to supply wood for the bows of the Scottish archers. Yet another freedom fighter is recalled in Wallace's Isle, at the mouth of the Inveruglas Water,

THE WATERS OF LOCH LOMOND are popular with all kinds of recreational users. Winter finds the moorings empty, and visitors few to Inchcailloch, part of the SNH National Nature Reserve.

THE VIEW SOUTH-WEST from the slopes of Ben Lomond.

BEN LOMOND (3195 ft / 974 m) (opposite), dominates views along the east shore of Loch Lomond. It is the most southerly of all the Munros – the 284 Scottish mountains over 3000 ft (914 m).

though whether or not the Scottish patriot ever sought refuge there seems uncertain.

Back on the east bank, the public road goes as far as Rowardennan. The substantial car park here is the starting point for a number of walks, including the ascent of Ben Lomond, Scotland's most southerly, and probably most popular, Munro. The path up Ben Lomond reflects its popularity, and was first marked on Ordnance Survey maps as early as the 1860s. For the less energetic, there are some fine waterfalls on the Ardess Burn, in the woodlands above Rowardennan.

Yet another option is to continue north on foot, using part of the West Highland Way. This traverses the fine oakwoods of Craigrostan, Rob Roy's

country, and inevitably, there are some MacGregor landmarks, notably a rocky outcrop falling sheer into the loch's waters. This is marked on maps as 'Rob Roy's Prison'. Legend has it he confined his enemies here, or dangled them in an unfriendly manner over the slabs.

Today, the east bank all along this section is a deserted spot, though eighteenth-century documents record that there were 150 families around the shores between Rowardennan and the north end of the loch. Nowadays, the woods belong to the birds and the wild goats which are frequently seen here. The Royal Society for the Protection of Birds has a reserve near Inversnaid, perhaps best sampled in late spring or early summer when the canopy of the

SO DEEP DID THE GLACIER cut in its channelling out of the Loch Lomond trench, that Loch Lomond lies out of sight between Loch Arklet, pictured here, and the sharp outlines of the 'Arrochar Alps', the distinctive mountain grouping on the west bank of Loch Lomond beyond Inveruglas.

oakwoods is at its noisiest with the song of warblers and other summer visitors.

Inversnaid on Loch Lomond can be visited by road from Aberfoyle via Loch Arklet. This loch sits in a 'hanging valley', that is, a glacial side valley at right-angles and to the east of the much deeper main Loch Lomond trench. Matching the glen in which Arklet sits is the glen which leads from Loch Sloy at the west, or Arrochar side, of Loch Lomond. Geologists point out that this suggests that a river formerly ran eastwards from somewhere near Loch Sloy and drained through towards Loch Katrine. With the last Ice Age this west-to-east system was cut by the powerful Loch Lomond glacier.

A waterfall is a typical hanging valley feature. The fall which flows from Arklet down to Loch Lomond at Inversnaid is much reduced from the time when the Wordsworths saw it, *en route* to Loch Katrine. Before the level of Loch Arklet was raised by a dam, in order for it to supply Loch Katrine, the Inversnaid waterfall must have run with greater force. Inversnaid itself was a little ferry house when the Wordsworths visited, while Loch Arklet was probably no more than an upland lochan with cultivated ground nearby, now submerged.

They climbed up the steep hill by the waterfall and into this hanging valley. There they saw 'a very large stone building… with a high wall round it, naked hill above, and neither field or tree near'. William said it was exactly like 'one of the spittals of the Alps'. In fact, as they were later to discover, it was a garrison, built after the 1715 Jacobite rebellion at the suggestion of the Duke of Montrose. He declared that the presence of government troops might deter the troublesome MacGregors. The same Duke had already been instrumental in having Rob Roy MacGregor declared an outlaw in 1712 and had seized his lands as security for unpaid debt. The lands included the site of the garrison – so it was small wonder that it was attacked and burned twice by the local MacGregors. Rob Roy himself is said to have led the first sortie against it. On the second occasion, this time around the beginning of the 1745 rebellion, Rob Roy was dead but his son James Mor and a cousin Gregor MacGregor of Glengyle actually captured the building with only a small party.

Even after the last Jacobite uprising, government forces continued to be garrisoned there, with the most famous commander of the troops stationed here being the future General Wolfe. By 1790, Sir Walter Scott recorded the post was down to a single veteran, while by the Wordsworths' 1803 visit, the place was occupied only by poor squatters. The scanty and ruinous remains are now part of a farm steading.

If the prospect eastward from the Loch Arklet garrison site is a shade dreary, the view across to the peaks of the Arrochar Alps on the west side of Loch Lomond is much more impressive. The wooded slopes above Loch Lomond, traversed by the famous travellers, are certainly a romantic spot. It was hereabouts that the Wordsworths encountered the charming local lass who inspired William's *To a Highland Girl. At Inversnayde upon Loch Lomond*. It contains the lines:

> *Sweet Highland Girl a very shower*
> *Of beauty is thy earthly dower.*

The girl in question was the sister of the Inversnaid ferryman and the site of her cottage must have been very near the present Inversnaid Hotel.

LOCH LOMOND'S EAST BANK (above) carries the route of the West Highland Way, a long-distance footpath. The peaceful east contrasts with the main road traffic on the loch's west side.

55

former days, the river was canalised as far as the Inverarnan Hotel for the convenience of steamer-borne visitors wishing refreshments. To the east a former cattle-droving route goes over the hills into Glen Gyle and Loch Katrine and is now little used even by walkers.

The west side of Loch Lomond differs greatly from the east bank. It carries main road traffic and, though road improvements have speeded up journey times, the main A82 is still a road which demands care as it snakes round the 'bonnie banks'. At the junction community of Tarbet, the sea makes its nearest approach to Loch Lomond, at the head of Loch Long.

There are other Tarbe(r)ts in Scotland, the word coming from the Gaelic meaning 'a place of portage of boats'. The most famous occasion when vessels were carried across the isthmus was in 1263 when King Haakon of Norway, in conflict with Scotland's King Alexander III, detached Olaf of Man with 60 ships from an even larger fleet anchored by the Cumbraes. The raiding force came up Loch Long and the boats were dragged the 2 miles (3 km) between the two lochs. Olaf swept the islands and the banks of the loch with his forces, at a time when they were said to be quite heavily populated. In the slaughter and conflagration it is likely that the little nunnery on Inchcailloch was sacked, along with the monastery in Inchtavannach, the hermitage on Island I Vow and all the little chapels at places like Glenmollachan and Rossdhu on the east shore.

Another noteworthy community on the west shore is the pretty village of Luss. This spot offers a fine view of Loch Lomond's islands, including Inchtavannach,

THE VILLAGE OF LUSS stands on the ancient clan lands of the Colquhouns where Glen Luss opens out on to Loch Lomondside. Only a little way above the Highland line, the hills west of the village are popular with walkers.

The same waterfall also inspired Gerard Manley Hopkins' poem *Inversnaid*, with its lines oft-quoted by the conservation movement:

> *What would the world be, once bereft*
> *Of wet and of wildness?*
> *Let them be left,*
> *Oh let them be left, wildness and wet;*
> *Long live the weeds and the wilderness yet.*

The final section of the east bank, to where Loch Lomond peters out by Ardlui, is also wild, and the West Highland Way takes the east side of the little hill Cnap Mor, which gives a superb view southwards down the winding length of the loch. The River Falloch runs into the loch below and to the west. In

which is really *innis tigh na mhanaich* – island of the monk's house, a reference to St Kessog. A shrine to this Celtic missionary was formerly sited near the village and the location became a place of pilgrimage. A medieval effigy of the saint can still be seen among local church relics, as can an ancient hogback tombstone and two early cross-slabs, all suggesting this was a site of religious importance.

For more than 750 years the settlement here has been associated with the Colquhouns, who acquired lands in the area during the fourteenth century. They were the hereditary guardians of the crozier of St Kessog. Generations later, in the early nineteenth century, the present Luss village was built, as part of the fashion for improvements which swept the land-owning classes at the time. It housed the estate's labourers, foresters and quarry workers. As a typical planned estate village, it has seen little change since then and is designated as an Outstanding Conservation Area.

It also has another life as the backdrop to the long-running television soap *Take the High Road*, as the fictional Glendarroch.

The name Luss is probably from the Gaelic *lios*, meaning 'a garden', though it is also associated with a local legend concerning a local baroness, married to a high-born French noble in the fourteenth century.

She died in France and was brought home for burial at Luss. Fleurs-de-lis (hence Luss) were cast on her grave, recalling her French connections. They grew and prospered and were later used to provide medication to counteract a pestilence. Or so the story goes. Whatever the truth, there are lots of gardens in Luss growing lilies, irises and roses.

Below Luss the Highland Boundary Fault is crossed once more, and the loch fans out, lapping the shores of the Balloch Country Park in the south. Centred on Balloch Castle, the local countryside ranger service helps interpret the precious recreational environment and there are displays on the wildlife of the area.

BALLOCH CASTLE COUNTRY PARK at the south end of Loch Lomond includes the grounds of Balloch Castle, a Scots Baronial style mansion house which houses the park's visitor centre.

LOOKING NORTH-WEST over the summit of Ben Lomond, this aerial view emphasises the narrow ribbon of Loch Lomond. Other glints of water come from Loch Sloy (centre), and a glimpse of the head of Loch Long (far left).

To the West & North of Loch Lomond

West of Loch Lomond looms a cluster of high tops. Perhaps slightly tongue in cheek, these are collectively sometimes referred to as the Arrochar Alps. When seen, for example, from the Loch Arklet road, looking west over the trench of Loch Lomond, their spiky appearance does give them an alpine profile.

These five rugged peaks form a half-circle to the north of the village of Arrochar. Ben Vorlich, Ben Ime, Ben Narnain and Ben Vane attract hillwalkers intent on bagging Munros, though it is the fifth which is the best known. Though 'The Cobbler' (which maps call Ben Arthur, though no-one else does) reaches only 2891 ft (881 m), its bumpy profile draws the eye from the head of Loch Long or from the West Highland Way across Loch Lomond. For all its stature, it actually offers more than seventy climbing pitches.

Loch Sloy is separated from Loch Lomond by the bulk of Ben Vorlich. The glen in which it lies was once the homelands of the Clan MacFarlane. 'Loch Sloy' was their war cry, though the ghost of any clansman returning today would see many changes. In 1946,

Italian prisoners of war, awaiting repatriation, were among the workers who built the 1170 ft (357 m) Loch Sloy dam, using 295,000 tons of crushed rock and concrete to a height of 182 ft (56 m). This drowned the old clan homelands for ever. It also explains the four large pipes which emerge from the Loch Lomond flank of Ben Vorlich to carry Sloy's water down to the Inveruglas Power Station. In spite of the power-line paraphernalia, a walk up the track to Loch Sloy still gives a worthwhile flavour of the rugged terrain.

Arrochar sits at the very end of Loch Long. Though the loch's name is an accurate description of this extraordinary fjord, 'long' in Gaelic really means 'ship'. Loch Long also abuts on to the Argyll Forest Park to the west and north. The Park's 52,630 acres (21,300 ha) offer a good range of forest walks, trails and picnic sites. Notable, for example, are the Cruaich Tairbeirt Woodland Walks, starting from the Arrochar and Tarbet railway station. They take in some impressive viewpoints over both Loch Long and the Cobbler, as well as Loch Lomond.

On its east bank, Loch Long meets the Rosneath peninsula. This area was close enough to Glasgow in Victorian times to attract the wealth of successful city business folk, many of whom built grand mansions and country retreats overlooking the salty waters of Loch Long or the Gare Loch to the east. Gothic and Scots baronial towers and roof-lines rise out of the greenery. Some are still in private hands, while others are hotels, but the loop round by Rosneath and Kilcreggan makes for interesting architecture as well as plenty of views of yachts at their moorings.

Glen Falloch shows the way up from the north end of Loch Lomond. Road and rail share the confines of the glen, which William Wordsworth described as 'the vale of awful sound', from the roaring of waterfalls such as the Ben-y-Glas Fall, which tumbles 120 ft (37 m). The gorge of the Black Water, in Gaelic the Dubh Eas, is also spectacular. The railway actually crosses here by a viaduct only a few feet short of the height of the track across the Forth Bridge, a reminder that the scenic West Highland Line is one of the best ways to see the area in comfort. It has been in the glen since 1894. The levelling out of the track at the head of the glen was formerly known as 'the fireman's rest', it being the first opportunity for the footplate man to straighten his back after 7 miles (11 km) of relentless shovelling to keep pressure up in the days of steam.

THE COBBLER (2891 ft / 881 m) With a ruggedness and character out of all proportion to its height, this mountain offers a variety of routes for rock climbers, though it can also be tackled by less adventurous hill walkers. It is usually referred to as Ben Arthur on maps.

THE CRIANLARICH HILLS from Ben Oss. (Ben More lies on the far right and Ben Chabhair on the left.) With seven Munros and fourteen tops, this is the highest group of hills south of Tayside. Ben More, at 3852 ft (1174 m), certainly justifies its translation from Gaelic simply as big hill.

There are also some southerly remnants of the old Caledonian pine forest in Glen Falloch, including one tree recently noted as being one of the very oldest in Scotland.

Road and rail reach the junction community of Crianlarich. At the meeting place of Glen Falloch, Glen Dochart and Strath Fillan, this is an old-established stopping-off point – raiding clansmen, cattle drovers and royalty have all passed this way. Crianlarich is also on the West Highland Way which then heads west up Strath Fillan. This area gets its name from Gaelic *srath*, a river plain or broad valley.

St Fillan was an early Irish missionary. His work in spreading Christianity throughout the Highlands is recalled by the very scanty remains of a twelfth-century priory founded in his name. This makes a pleasant walk along part of the West Highland Way by Kirkton Farm, north-west of the main road. There are excellent views from this section towards Ben Lui.

A little further west, another junction community, Tyndrum, also marks the western end of the uplands of Breadalbane, as this great northerly swathe of hill country is called. The 'high grounds of Scotland' make Tyndrum and Crianlarich especially good bases for hillwalkers. Tyndrum is notable in Highland communities in that it has, uniquely, two railway stations, upper and lower. Before that, it lay on Caulfeild's military road of 1750-2 and, in parallel with other places in the wider area, like Strathyre and Callander, was an important droving stance.

Tyndrum has one other notable association in that it had a lead mining industry from 1739 to 1798 under Sir Robert Clifton (the village used to be called Clifton). The mines reopened in 1838 for a further 30 years. The workings can still be made out on Meall Odhar, west of the village. Today, the quartz veins which attracted these early miners because of their lead content are being investigated by modern gold prospectors on the slopes of Ben Lui.

Amongst the Towns

With names so famed in scenic terms like the Trossachs and Loch Lomond, the urban face of the area can sometimes be neglected. Nevertheless, there are a number of towns with interesting historical or architectural backgrounds. Minutes from Loch Lomond where the short River Leven reaches the widening Clyde is the ancient settlement of Dumbarton. Guarding the Clyde approaches, the town here owes its origin to a fortified rock. It is thought that the craggy heights of Dumbarton Rock (the core of an ancient volcano), is the oldest continually fortified site in Scotland. Once it was the headquarters of the ancient Scottish kingdom of the North Britons, a Pictish tribe, so that Dumbarton is really Dun-Briton - 'the fort of the Britons'.

The early works on the Rock have also greatly altered through the years, with earlier medieval fortifications obliterated by the positioning of batteries from the sixteenth century onwards. However, visitors can still see a twelfth-century gateway and a sundial dating from the sixteenth century, gifted by Mary, Queen of Scots.

For long a shipbuilding centre, the most famous vessel launched here was probably the noted clipper *Cutty Sark*. The shipbuilding family of Denny, as major employers until well into the present century, became major benefactors in the town. Today's visitors can also see the unique Denny Ship Model Experiment Tank, where for more than a hundred years, models of new designs for hulls were tested before the real thing was built.

Minutes away, and also facing Clyde's water, is a town with a different history. Far from an ancient origin and an industrial past, Helensburgh owes its beginnings to the plans for improvement put into practice by Sir James Colquhoun, 8th Baronet of Colquhoun and Luss. He founded a new settlement here in 1776, intending it to be a weaving community. He named his new town Helensburgh, after his wife, Lady Helen Colquhoun. When it failed to attract industry, Colquhoun changed his plans and advertised it as a potential residential town of quality. He was soon aided by rapid advances in communications and the development of the steam engine (both for boats and railways). Soon a grid plan had evolved with spacious streets laid out on the slopes above the shore.

Its first provost (Scots: mayor) was Henry Bell in

THE FORTH & CLYDE CANAL, partially opened by 1773, remained in use for commerce until 1962. Today, it offers pleasant walking for much of its length.

The Forth Valley, east of Stirling, also has many points of interest in its towns. The historic development of Alloa was for long tied up with the Erskines, the Earls of Mar, whose seat Alloa Tower, survives today, though greatly altered. Under their patronage, the town became an important brewing, glass-making and textile centre.

Distilling also was important, with distilleries at Kennetpans and Kilbagie, south-east of Alloa, amongst the largest in Scotland before the end of the eighteenth century.

Nearby Clackmannan is a town with a past lost in legend. Like Edinburgh and Stirling, it grew up around a castle on a high point. The castle is the neglected Clackmannan Tower, originally dating from the fourteenth century. *Clach* is Gaelic for stone and Clackmannan, the former county town, may mean stone of Mannan, who was a Celtic sea god (as in Isle of Man). The stone in particular sits on top of another upright stone beside the Tolbooth. Alternatively Clackmannan means Stone of the Manau, a local tribe in the Iron Age.

Across the Forth is the major industrial centre of Falkirk, associated with early developments in the Industrial Revolution, thanks to its local sources of coal and iron. Today, points of interest in Falkirk include Callendar House, a mansion set in attractive parkland. Its story goes back 900 years and it has connections with Mary, Queen of Scots. Servants in period dress bring to life a working kitchen of the 1820s. Also within easy reach is the Bo'ness and Kinneil Railway, a nostalgic evocation of a Scottish branch line in the days of steam.

CLACKMANNAN TOLBOOTH & MAIN STREET,
The belfry tower, pictured here, is all that survives of the original tolbooth, built in the late 16th century.

ALLOA TOWER (opposite), was originally built in 1497 and is the only remaining part of the ancestral home of the Earls of Mar.

1807. His name is usually associated with the development of steam navigation, as the first man to use a practical steamboat in regular service, the *Comet*. It was launched in 1812 and ran regular trips from Glasgow to Helensburgh – the first steam-powered vessel on a public service in Europe, 13 years ahead of the first public railway. Bell had every reason to make this project successful as he owned a hotel in the town.

Helensburgh today is sometimes called 'a museum of villas'. Probably the most famous building in the town is the Hill House, considered to be the finest of the Scottish architect Charles Rennie Mackintosh's domestic designs. It was built for the publisher W.W. Blackie in 1902-3 and contains many original Mackintosh fittings and furniture. It is in the care of the National Trust for Scotland.

INDEX

*Entries in **bold** indicate pictures*

First published in Great Britain in 1999 by
Lomond Books, 36 West Shore Road, Granton, Edinburgh EH5 1QD
Produced by Colin Baxter Photography Ltd

Photographs Copyright © Colin Baxter 1999
Text Copyright © Colin Baxter Photography Ltd 1999
All rights reserved

A CIP record for this book
is available from the British Library

ISBN 0 947782 12 5

Printed in Hong Kong

Front cover photograph: *LOCH KATRINE AT DUSK*
Page 1 photograph: *STIRLING CASTLE*
Back cover photograph: *NATIONAL WALLACE MONUMENT AND THE OCHIL HILLS*